## First Facts
# Under the Sea

Written by Chris Madsen
Illustrated by Mike Lacey

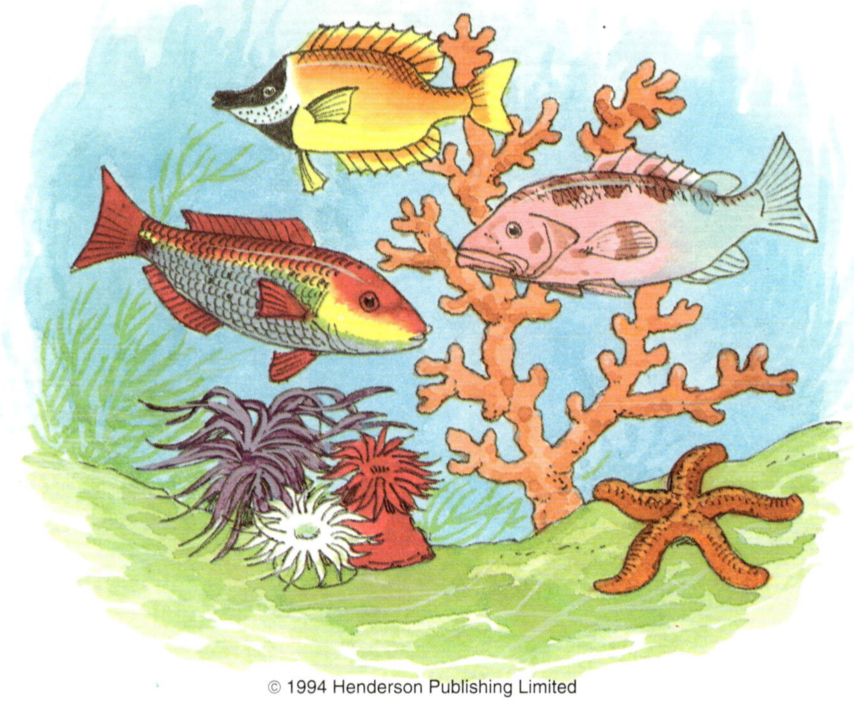

© 1994 Henderson Publishing Limited

Woodbridge, England

# The Sea

This is a picture of the Earth taken from space. The white fluffy bits are clouds. The brown shapes are land. The rest is masses of dark blue sea.

Only a quarter of the Earth is covered by land. The other three quarters is covered by the sea. This is three times more than the amount covered by land.

The sea stretches for miles. It is often thousands of metres deep. We still do not know very much about life underwater. Exploring is very difficult. It costs a lot of money.

The sea is the only place left on Earth that people have not been able to explore properly.

UNDER THE SEA 3

# The Oceans

There are five great oceans in the world. Look at the map and see if you can find them.

**Arctic Ocean**
**Atlantic Ocean**
**Pacific Ocean**
**Indian Ocean**
**Southern Ocean**

Seas are smaller than the oceans and they are not as deep. Can you find these seas on the map?

**Mediterranean Sea**
**North Sea**
**Red Sea**
**Caribbean Sea**
**Tasman Sea**

Can you see where you live on the map?

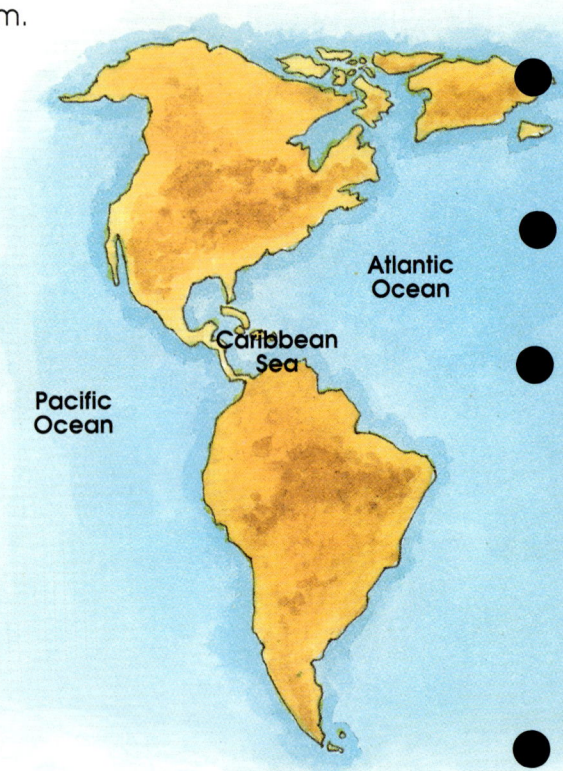

## Why is the sea salty?

Rainwater falls on the land. Salt in the rocks dissolves in the rainwater.

This water flows into streams. Streams flow into rivers. Rivers flow into the sea.

The salt collects in the sea.

4  UNDER THE SEA

Arctic Ocean

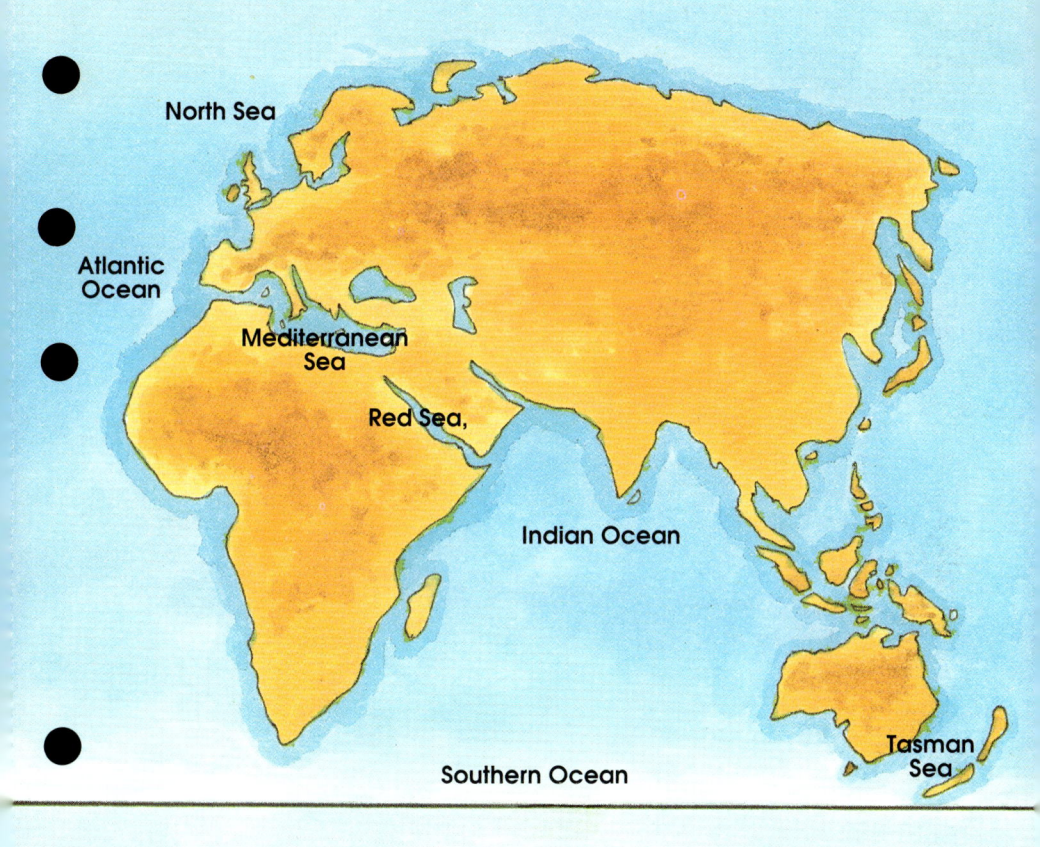

North Sea

Atlantic Ocean

Mediterranean Sea

Red Sea

Indian Ocean

Tasman Sea

Southern Ocean

UNDER THE SEA 5

# The Land Under the Sea

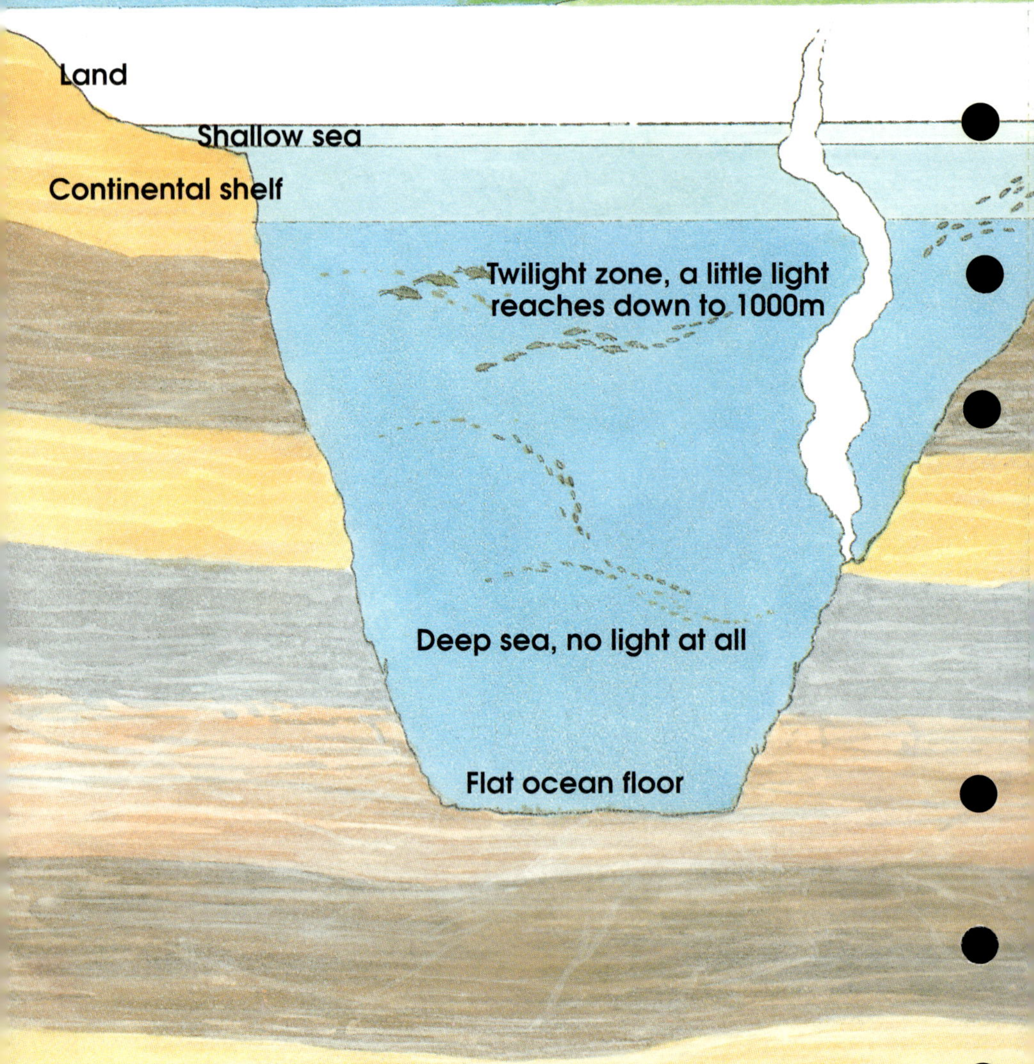

Land

Shallow sea

Continental shelf

Twilight zone, a little light reaches down to 1000m

Deep sea, no light at all

Flat ocean floor

The shape of the sea bed looks like the land. There are underwater mountains, valleys, flat open plains and tall cliffs. There are even volcanoes and landslides. Strong currents flow across the sea bed like rivers crossing the land.

6  UNDER THE SEA

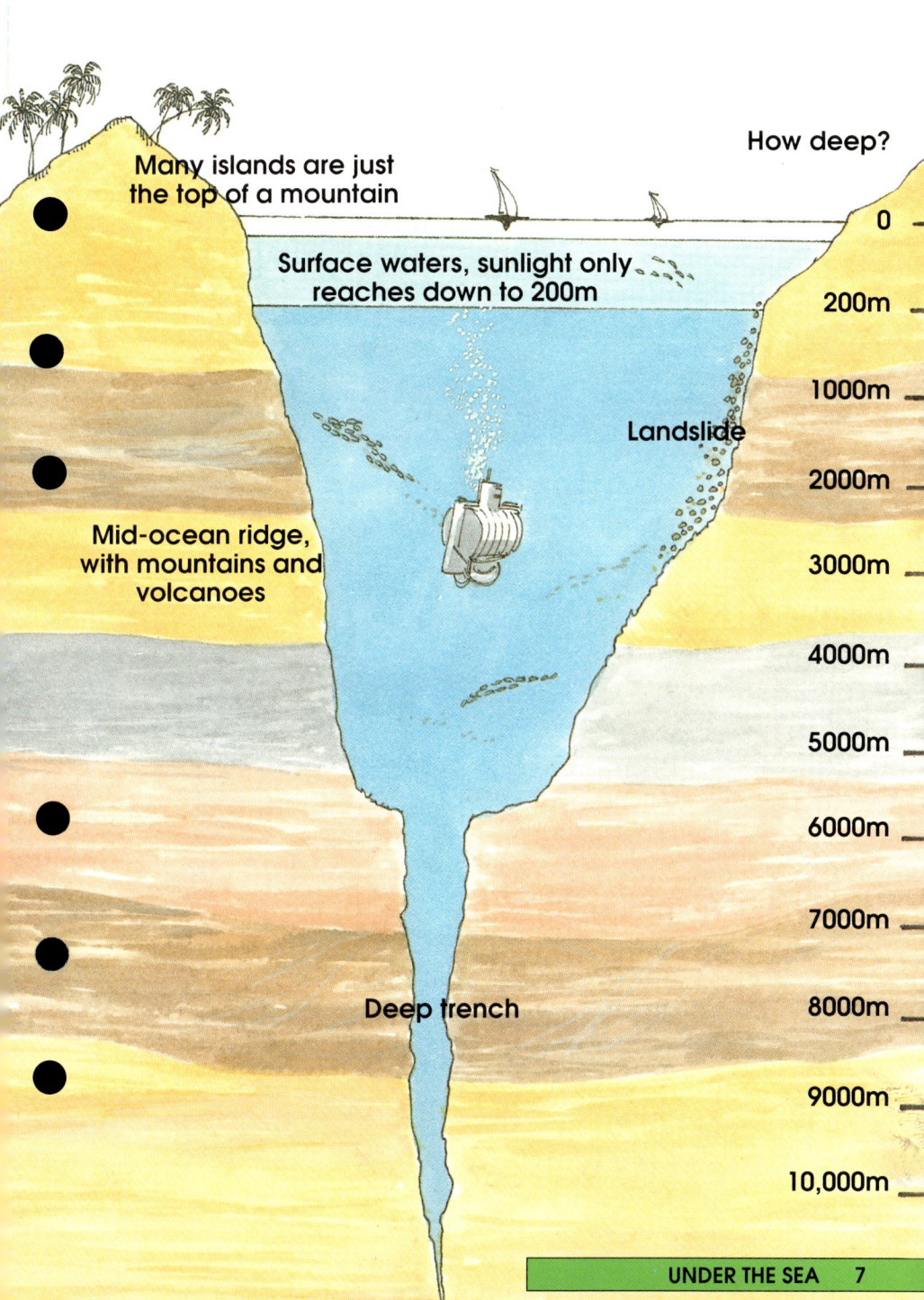

# Floaters

The surface of the sea is light and sunny. Many animals and plants spend all their lives just floating in the top few metres of the water. These floating animals and plants are called plankton.

The plankton is the food factory of the sea. Tiny, microscopic plants, called algae, trap energy from the sun. They change the sun's energy into foods like sugar.

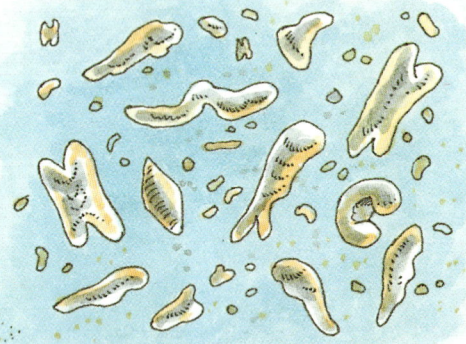

Animals get their energy by eating the algae or other animals. There are many small animals in the plankton.

Nothing is wasted. Bits of dead animals and plants sink down and are eaten by animals living in the sea bed.

Some planktonic animals are large:

**Common Jellyfish** are often seen in the harbours.

The **By-the-Wind-Sailor** has a sail and is blown along by the wind.

**Portuguese Man-O-War** has long tentacles.

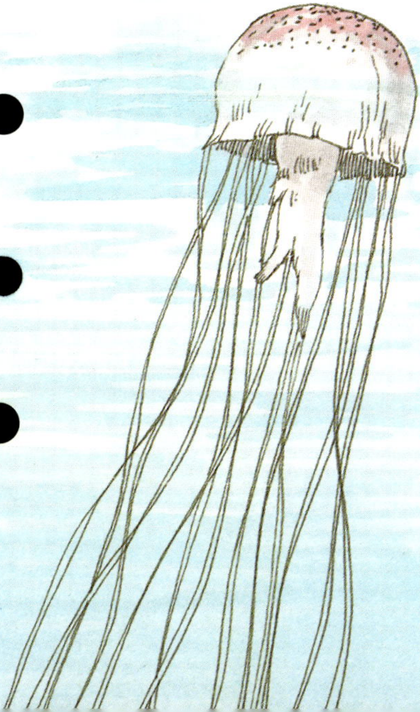

**Goose Barnacles** hang down from a float or a piece of wood.

# Swimmers

Millions of fish swim in the open sea. They often swim together in a huge shoal. A shoal is a large group of fish, all swimming together. It helps to protect them from bigger fish that try to eat them.

These fish are caught by fishermen for us to eat:

Mackerel

Herring

Haddock

Cod

Tuna

Anchovy

**Tuna** are large fish. They live in warmer waters and swim very fast.

10  UNDER THE SEA

Some strange fish:

The **Swordfish** has a long sword to cut into shoals of fish.

**Flying fish** jump out of the water and fly. They use their fins like wings.

**Eels** have a long thin body like a snake.

**Sunfish** are huge round fish. They often float on the surface of the sea.

In the deepest seas it is dark all the time. Some very unusual fish live here. Some have lights on their bodies. Others have huge eyes and mouths.

Angler-fish

UNDER THE SEA  11

# Sharks

Sharks are large predators. This means that they catch other animals and eat them. Sharks have rows of very sharp teeth. Each one is shaped like a triangle.

The biggest sharks are gentle plankton feeders. The **Basking Shark** grows up to 13m long. The **Whale Shark** grows up to 18m long. The **Blue Shark** catches small fish.

Whale Shark

Basking Shark

Blue Shark

The **Great White Shark** is the most dangerous. They sometimes attack people.

Great White Shark

**Skates** and **Rays** have wide flat bodies. They live on the sea bed.

Skate

Dogfish

**Dogfish** are small sharks that live on sand banks.

# Whales

Whales are not fish. They are warm-blooded animals, just like people, dogs and cats.

- The **Blue Whale** is the biggest animal ever to have lived on Earth. It grows up to 30m long and feeds on plankton.

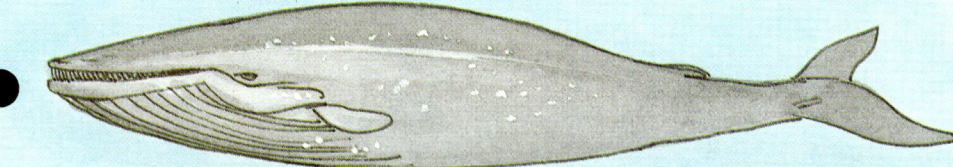

- **Humpback Whales** sing to each other.

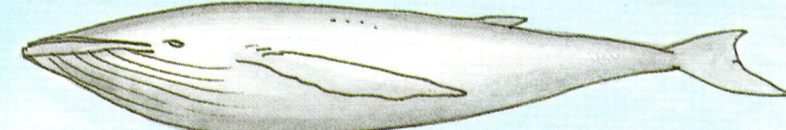

- **Dolphins** and **Porpoises** are small whales. They often swim next to ships.

- Whales used to be killed to give meat and oil. Today many whales are so rare, they may become extinct. This means that they will be dead and gone forever.

- **Sperm Whales** dive deep down into the ocean to catch **Giant Squid**. This animal is like a huge octopus.

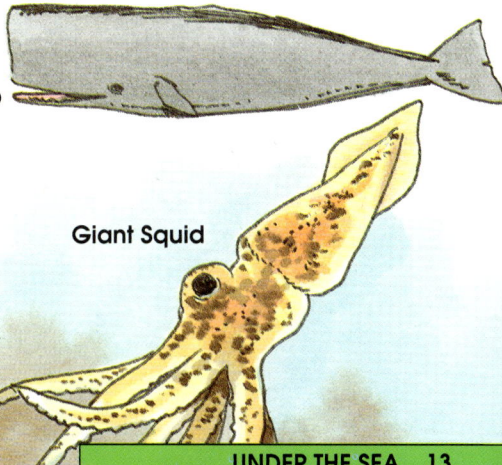

Giant Squid

UNDER THE SEA 13

# Crawlers

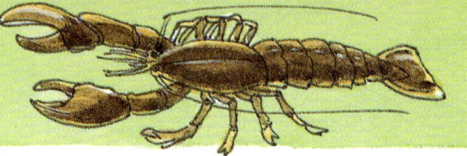

Down at the bottom of the sea, many animals crawl, swim or wriggle over the sea bed.

**Shrimps**, **Crabs** and **Lobsters** have long walking legs. The first pair of legs are large nippers. They use them to tear up food and for fighting.

Flatfish like **Plaice** and **Sole** live on the sea bed.

The **Angler Fish** is very ugly. It holds a fin, like a fishing rod, over it's huge mouth. Other fish come to look at the rod and are snapped into the angler fish's mouth.

The **Octopus** uses it's eight legs to crawl over the rocks. It swims away when danger is near.

Many other small animals crawl over the rocks or sand.

UNDER THE SEA

# Stickers

Stickers spend most of their life stuck to the hard surface of rocks. If they cannot find a rock to grow on, then they will grow on the bottom of a ship, a pier or something else man-made.

Seaweed grows in shallow water. **Bladder Wrack** grows at the water's edge. **Kelps** are found deeper down. They form great forests of seaweed in some parts of the world.

Lots of different animals are stickers. Many do not move once they have settled in one place. Others move a little bit, but go back to the same home.

**Barnacles** are a sort of shrimp-type animal. They live inside a hard chalky shell which is firmly stuck to a rock. They catch pieces of food that float past. **Tube Worms** also live in a chalky tube, stuck to a rock. **Limpets** are snails that have a simple, cone-shaped shell. They cling onto rocks with their very strong foot. It is like a bigger sucker. **Chitons** have a shell made up of several pieces.

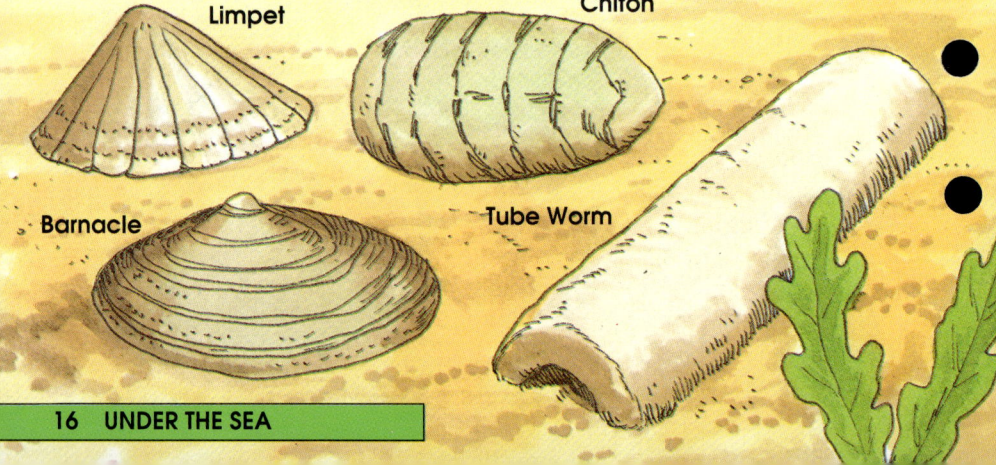

**Sea Anemones** look like flowers. Food is caught on their tentacles and pushed into their mouth.

Sponges

Sea Anemones

**Sponges** grow over rocks. They form lots of different shapes. Some look like plants, others look like a bath sponge.

Lumpsucker

The **Lumpsucker** is a strange fish that has a sucker to stick itself onto rocks.

Mussel

Oyster

**Mussels** use very strong threads to cling onto rocks. **Oysters** stick one of their shells to a rock or stone.

Remora

The **Remora** has a large sucker on it's head which it uses to stick onto large fish. It hitches a ride and eats scraps of food from the fish's dinner. They live in warm seas.

UNDER THE SEA 17

# Burrowers

These animals live in a burrow, which is a long tunnel that they dig into soft sand and mud. Some stay in the burrow all of the time. Others leave it to go and hunt for food on the sea bed.

Most worms and clams are burrowers.

They feed by sucking water into their tunnel. Tiny pieces of food are strained out of the water.

burrowing clams

burrowing worms

Cockle

Razor Shell

Auger Shell

18  UNDER THE SEA

# Coral Reef

Coral only grows in warm waters. The water has to be shallow and very clean.

Each coral is a colony of tiny animals all living together. The animals are like sea anemones. They are polyps. They build themselves a hard, rocky skeleton. It is a bit like lots of people building a city, or lots of ants building an ant's nest. Coral comes in all sorts of shapes and sizes.

Corals grow on top of each other and eventually form a rocky reef. Reefs form along the coast of many tropical islands. The largest reef is the Great Barrier Reef, Australia.

Here are some of the many pretty animals that live on a coral reef.

The **Crown of Thorns Starfish** is not very welcome. It eats coral and is killing large parts of the Great Barrier Reef.

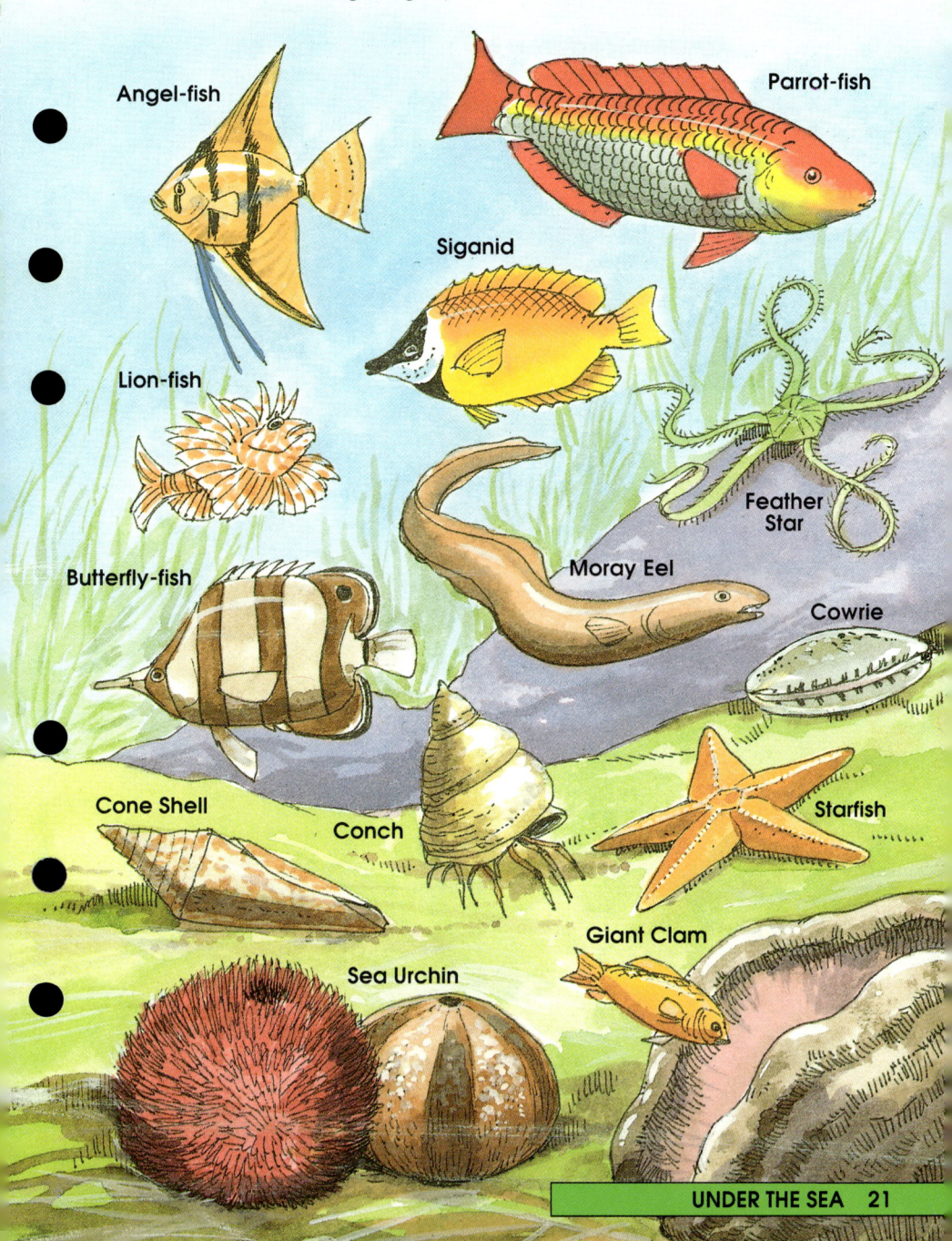

# Under the Ice

The North Pole is covered by the Arctic Ocean. But because it is so cold, the sea has frozen. It is covered with a thick sheet of ice. The ice is 3000m thick. But the ice does not reach all the way down to the sea bed, so submarines and fish can pass underneath.

The **Polar Bear** is the only bear that lives in the sea. It lives on the ice flows and can swim from one iceberg to the next. It's thick fur keeps it warm. Polar Bears are only found in the Arctic.

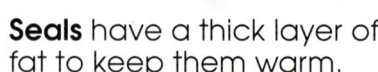

**Seals** have a thick layer of fat to keep them warm.

**Walruses** have long tusks and strong bristles around their mouth. They use them to find clams that are buried in the sea bed.

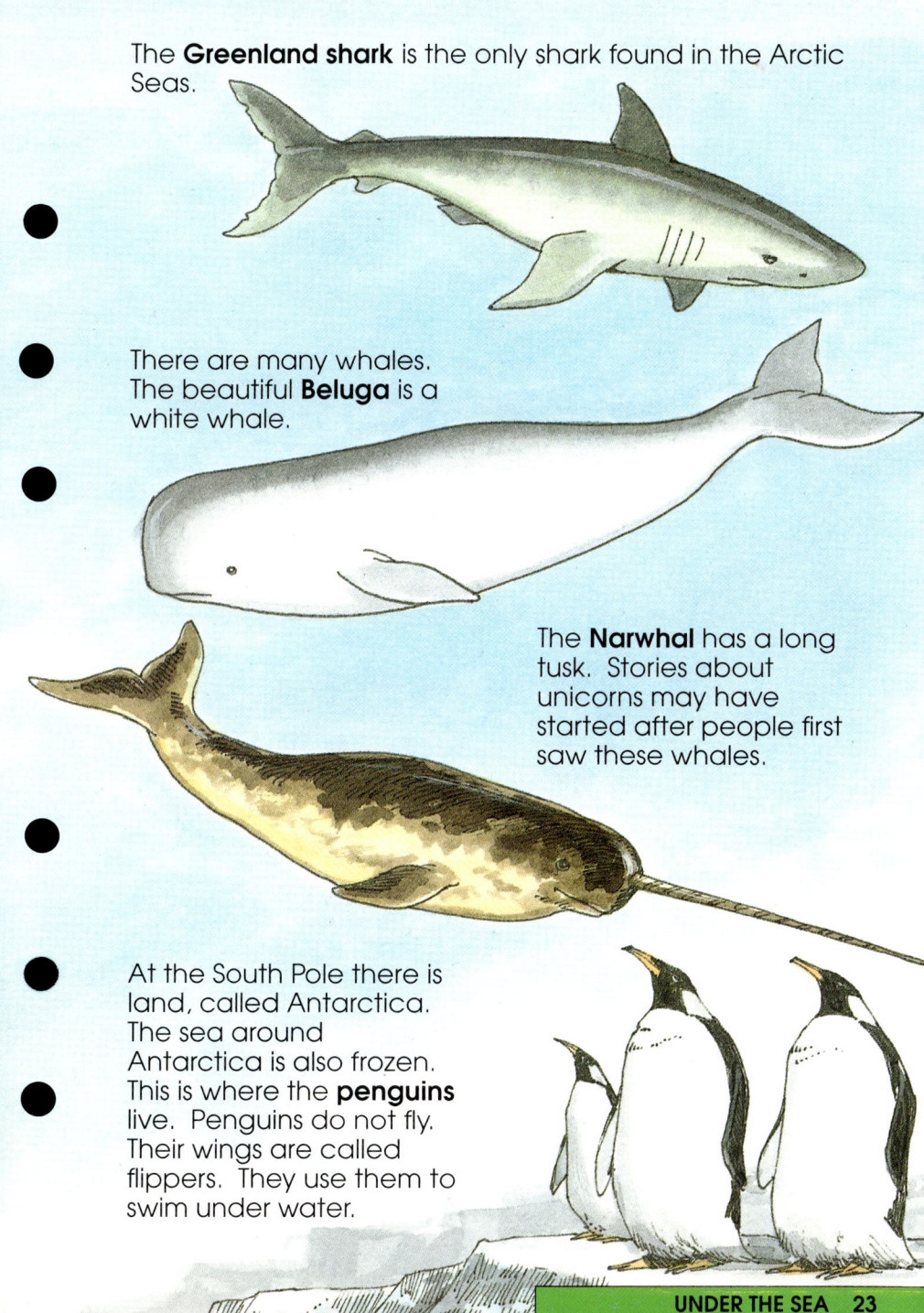

The **Greenland shark** is the only shark found in the Arctic Seas.

There are many whales. The beautiful **Beluga** is a white whale.

The **Narwhal** has a long tusk. Stories about unicorns may have started after people first saw these whales.

At the South Pole there is land, called Antarctica. The sea around Antarctica is also frozen. This is where the **penguins** live. Penguins do not fly. Their wings are called flippers. They use them to swim under water.

UNDER THE SEA    23

# Food from the Sea

Man has been fishing in the sea for thousands of years.

Today, modern fishing equipment helps the fishermen to find huge shoals of fish. Enormous **purse seine nets** surround the shoal and scoop all the fish up in one go.

Flat fish and shellfish are caught with a **trawl net**.

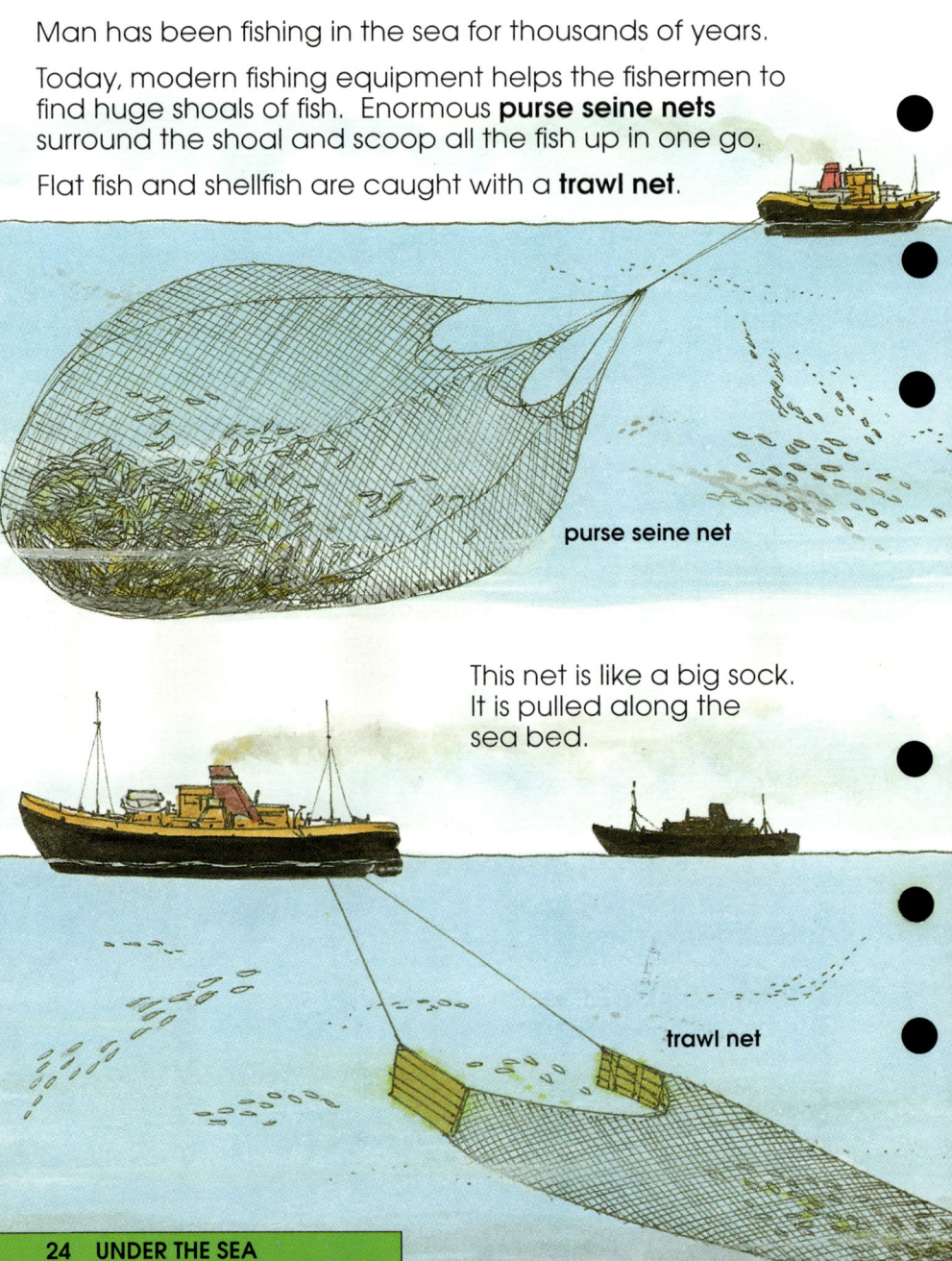

purse seine net

This net is like a big sock. It is pulled along the sea bed.

trawl net

Very long **drift nets** hang down in the sea like a huge curtain. Fish swim into them and are caught. But other animals are caught in these nets as well. Whales, dolphins, turtles and birds are all killed.

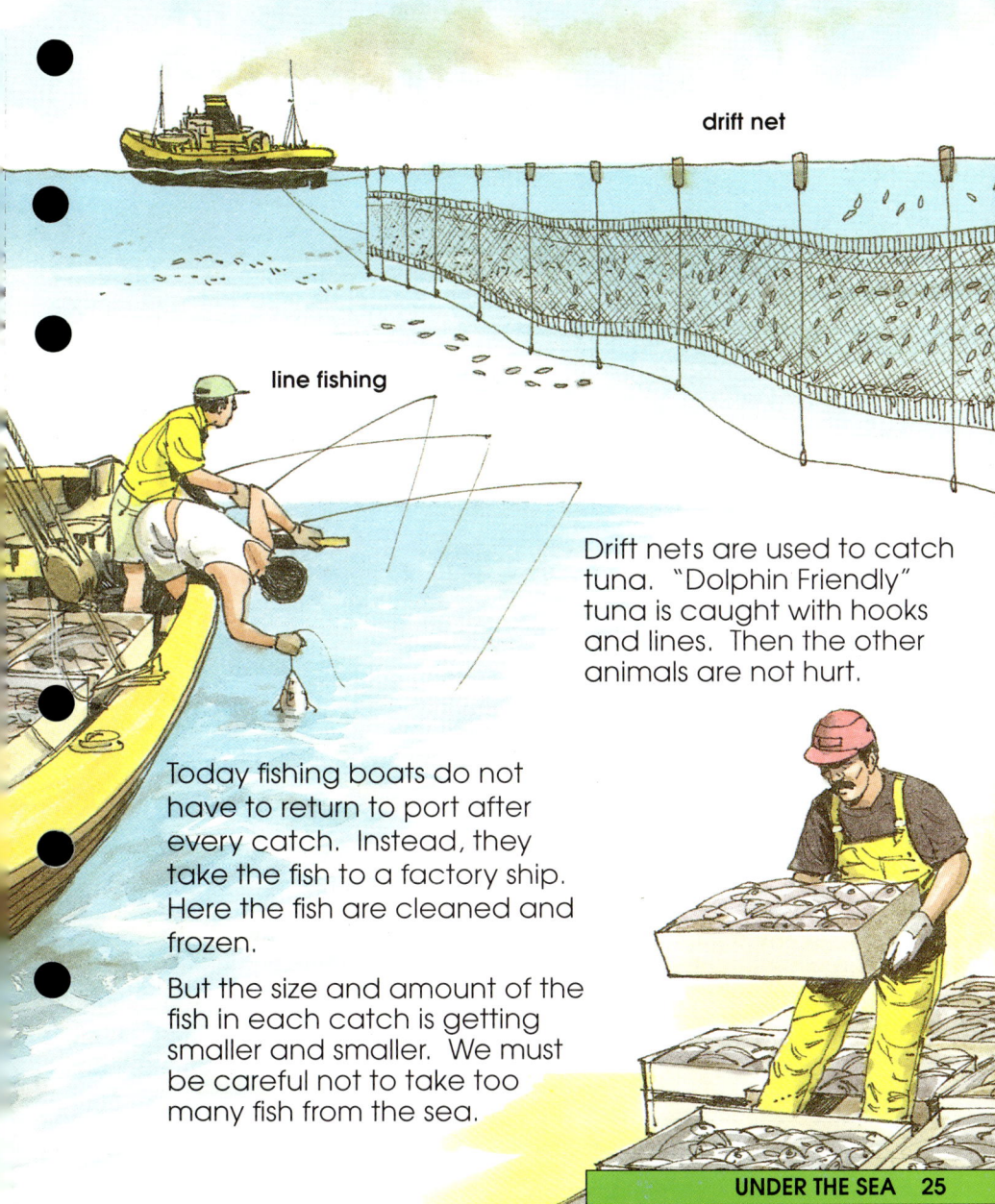

drift net

line fishing

Drift nets are used to catch tuna. "Dolphin Friendly" tuna is caught with hooks and lines. Then the other animals are not hurt.

Today fishing boats do not have to return to port after every catch. Instead, they take the fish to a factory ship. Here the fish are cleaned and frozen.

But the size and amount of the fish in each catch is getting smaller and smaller. We must be careful not to take too many fish from the sea.

UNDER THE SEA

# Man Under the Sea

People cannot breathe under water, so they need special equipment if they want to stay under the water.

## Diving

Divers use an aqualung. This is a tank of compressed air. The diver breathes the air through a mouthpiece. Divers wear flippers on their feet to help them to swim. A belt with heavy weights helps to keep them under water. A rubber suit keeps them warm. Divers wear a face mask to help them see underwater.

UNDER THE SEA

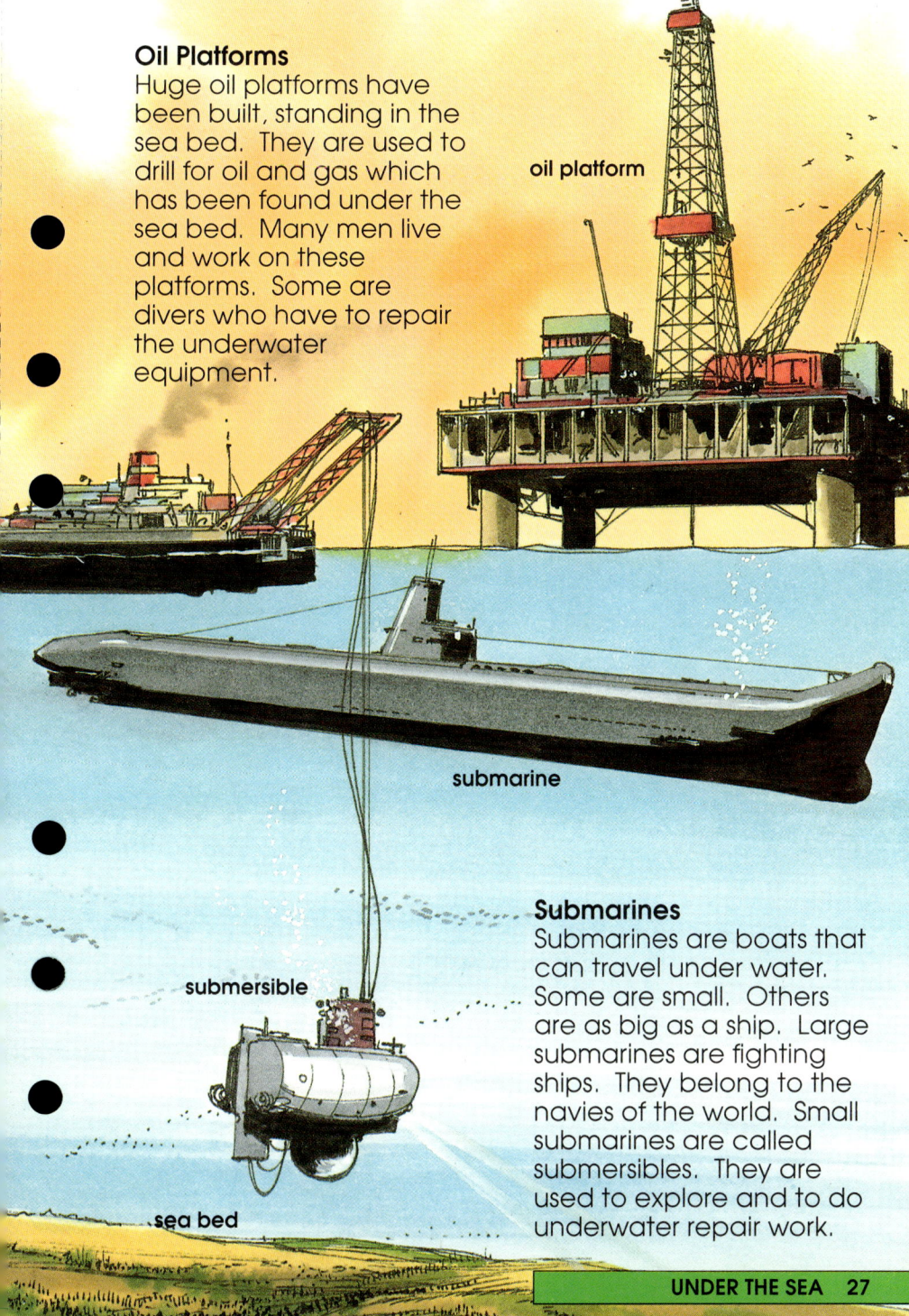

## Oil Platforms

Huge oil platforms have been built, standing in the sea bed. They are used to drill for oil and gas which has been found under the sea bed. Many men live and work on these platforms. Some are divers who have to repair the underwater equipment.

## Submarines

Submarines are boats that can travel under water. Some are small. Others are as big as a ship. Large submarines are fighting ships. They belong to the navies of the world. Small submarines are called submersibles. They are used to explore and to do underwater repair work.

UNDER THE SEA 27

# Ship Wrecks

Many ships have been wrecked and now lie at the bottom of the sea. Here are two famous ones:

## Mary Rose

This ship was the flagship of Henry VIII's navy. In 1545 she sailed from Portsmouth, in England, to fight the French navy who were attacking the town. Suddenly, as she changed direction, she tipped over. The water rushed in through her open gun ports and she sank. Nearly everybody on board was killed.

The wreck of the Mary Rose was discovered by divers in 1971. The site was carefully studied for many years.

In 1982, the Mary Rose was brought back up to the surface. She was taken back to Portsmouth, 437 years after she left. She is now in a museum.

## Titanic

When she was built, they said the Titanic could not sink. But in 1912, she left Southampton in England, to make her first journey to America. We call this a 'maiden voyage'.

Halfway across the Atlantic, she hit an iceberg. Water came in through the hole in the ship's side and she sank. Nearly 1500 people were killed.

Many people searched for the wreck of the Titanic. It was found in 1985 by submersibles carrying cameras and other equipment. They searched the sea bed near to where the ship sank. The Titanic lies 4000m down, at the bottom of the Atlantic Ocean. She has been photographed, but nothing can be brought up to the surface.

# Spot-It Sea Life

You do not always have to be under the sea to spot sea life. See how many of the things below you can spot on the seashore.

**Razor Shell** in the sand or in rock pools

**Limpet** stuck on rocks and in rock pools

**Mussels** in clumps attached to rocks

**Jellyfish** washed up on the beach or in rock pools

**Bladder Wrack** seaweed can be found on the beach, or in the water

**Starfish** in rock pools or on the beach

**Urchin** in rock pools

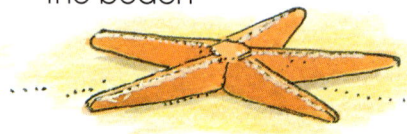

**Crab** in the sand or rock pools

**Seal** swimming in the sea or basking on sand banks

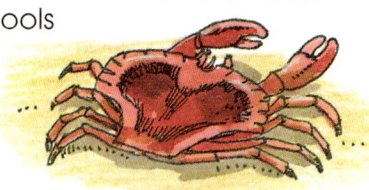

**Coralline** another seaweed to be found on the beach or in the water

# Funny Names

Many animals in the sea have strange names. Can you guess what these animals are? Answers on page 32.

1. ★ + fish = Starfish
2. sea + potato = Sea pocaToe
3. sea + slug = Seaslug
4. feather + star = fethrStar
5. sun + fish = Sunfish
6. parrot + fish = parroefish
7. jelly + fish = jellyfish

# What does that word mean?

**algae** — a simple plant

**clam** — shellfish, their body is covered with two shells that close tightly together

**compressed air** — air that is squashed into a small space

**microscopic** — something so small, that you need a microscope to see it with

**plankton** — animals and plants that float in the sea

**predator** — an animal that eats other animals

**tentacle** — a long soft, bendy feeler

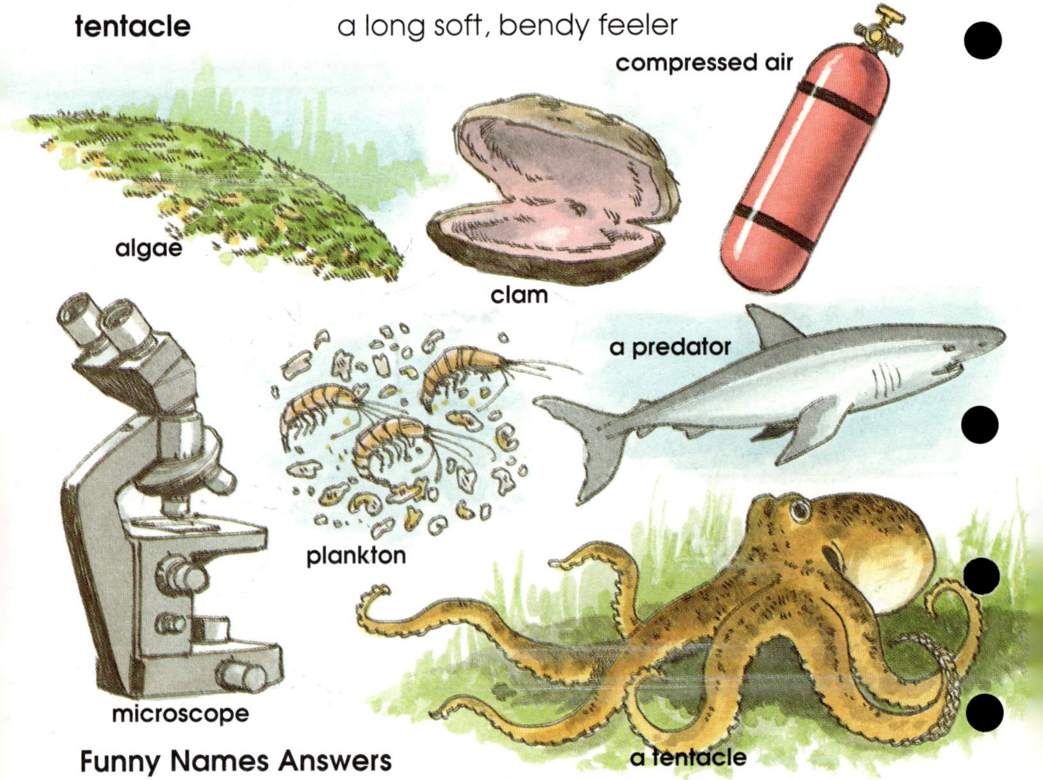

compressed air

algae

clam

a predator

plankton

microscope

a tentacle

## Funny Names Answers

1. Starfish
2. Sea Potato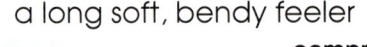
3. Sea Slug
4. Feather Star
5. Sun Fish
6. Parrot-fish
7. Jellyfish

32  UNDER THE SEA

# More  Titles

Dot-to-Dot Dinosaurs
My First Joke Book
Number Fun
Animal Families Sticker Colouring
Picture Puzzles
First Facts Castles
Winter Fun
Save Our World Copy Colouring
Funny Faces Sticker Fun
Start to Draw
Look Out For Creepy Crawlies
First Facts People and Places
Animal World Night Animals
Summer Fun
First Atlas
Look Out For Seashore Life
First Facts Our World
Stick-a-Story Gulliver's Travels

## The Children's Organiser

# JUNIOR FUN FAX ™

## The Children's Organiser

We hope you will enjoy all the books in the JUNIOR FUNFAX series just as they are. But if you have a Junior Funfax Organiser, you can keep these pages inside. Each page has been drilled with six holes so you can remove the book cover and fit the pages into your own Organiser.

### FIRST FACTS
### UNDER THE SEA

If you could look under the waves, what a wonderful sight you would see. Strange plants and flowers, deep caves and fish, all shapes and sizes. Tiny fish and monster fish, stripy fish, spotted fish, in every colour and pattern. You will discover a living rainbow inside this book.

© 1993 Henderson Publishing Limited

ISBN 1-85597-178-X

*Henderson Publishing*
Woodbridge, England

£1.50